Exploring Emotions with Emory

By:
Monique R. Simpson, LCSW

Copyright @2021 by Monique Simpson

All rights reserved. No part of this publication may be reproduced, stored in a retrieval system, or transmitted in any form or by any means electronic, mechanical, photocopying, recording, or otherwise without the written permission of the authors.

Limits of Liability-Disclaimer

The authors and publisher shall not be liable for your misuse of this material. The purpose of this book is to educate and empower. The authors and/or publisher do not guarantee that anyone following these techniques, suggestions, tips, ideas, and/or strategies will become successful.

The authors and/or publisher shall have neither liability nor responsibility to anyone with respect to any loss or damage caused or alleged to be caused directly or indirectly by the information contained in this book.

ISBN: 978-1-7363669-2-9
Publisher: InspiredByVanessa

Dedication

This book is dedicated to blended families all over the world. Whether it is sibling rivalry, co-parenting, stepparent discipline styles, creating bonds, or finding a new balance, adjusting to life changes takes time, but it is always worth it!

Illustrated by: Jessi Bordi

What are Emotions?

Emotions are how we feel and respond to things that we experience.

> **Children often do not know the words to express how they feel, so they act out emotions inappropriately.**

Let's Explore Your Emotions!

What is Anger?

A strong feeling of displeasure toward someone or something.

This is Emory's angry face.

Emory feels angry when she believes something is unfair.

What makes you angry?

Draw your angry face.

What is Frustration?

The feeling of discouragement, anger, and annoyance because of unresolved problems or unfilled goals, desires, or needs.

This is Emory's frustrated face.

Emory often becomes frustrated when she is unsuccessful in completing a task.

What makes you frustrated?

Draw your frustrated face.

What is Hurt (Feelings)?

Unhappiness or sadness caused by someone's words or actions.

This is Emory's hurt face.

Emory's feelings are hurt when family or friends are not nice to her.

What makes you feel hurt?

Draw your hurt face.

What is Sadness?

The expression of grief or unhappiness.

This is Emory's sad face.

Emory is sad when she has to leave family and friends, when she loses things, or when she is unable to do the things she enjoys.

What makes you feel sad?

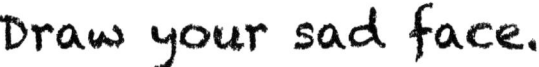

What is Scared?

Being in a state of fear, fright, or panic.

This is Emory's scared face.

Emory is scared of dogs and bugs.

What makes you feel scared?

Draw your sad face.

What is Nervousness?

Easily becoming worried, frightened, or anxious.

This is Emory's nervous face.

Emory is nervous when she has to perform dance and cheer routines.

What makes you feel nervous?

Draw your sad face.

What is Happiness?

Enjoying or characterized by well-being and contentment.

This is Emory's happy face.

Emory is happy when she spends time with her cousins, her grandparents, and when she helps her mom to cook.

What makes you feel happy?

Draw your happy face.

What is Excitement?

> Having, showing, or characterized by a heightened state of energy, enthusiasm, or eagerness.

This is Emory's Excited face.

Emory is excited when she tries new things and goes to new places.

What makes you feel excited?

What is Pride?

Having or displaying excessive self-esteem.

This is Emory's proud face.

Emory feels proud when she accomplishes a task.

What makes you feel proud?

Draw your proud face.

What is Love?

Strong affection or likeness for another.

This is Emory's loved face.

Emory feels loved by her family and friends for all their support.

What makes you feel loved?

Draw your loved face.

We have explored many emotions, but there are many more to go.

Emotional intelligence is the goal we want to accomplish as we grow!

Thank you for exploring with me!

CERTIFICATE OF COMPLETION

_____

Name

HAS COMPLETED

EXPLORING EMOTIONS WITH EMORY

About the Authors

The authors, Monique Simpson, LCSW, and Emory Hatchett, are mother and daughter who share a wonderful dynamic. Emory is a beautiful 6-year-old girl with an exuberant personality. She loves family, friends, and FOOD!

Monique is a graduate of Norfolk State University, a Licensed Clinical Social Worker, owner/psychotherapist of EMORY Center for Counseling and Wellness, and a member of Delta Sigma Theta Sorority, Inc. Both Emory and Monique enjoy quality time together with tons of laughter.

Please feel free to stay in contact with Monique at:

Email: Monique@emoryccw.com
Instagram: www.Instagram.com/emory.ccw
Instagram: www.Instagram.com/emorymonique

Works Cited

Merriam-Webster, Incorporated (2020). Anger, Frustrated, Hurt, Sadness, Scared, Nervous, Happy, Excited, Proud, Loved. Accessed June 26, 2020, through https://www.merriam-webster.com/

www.ingramcontent.com/pod-product-compliance
Lightning Source LLC
Chambersburg PA
CBHW061358090426
42743CB00002B/63